THE LITTLE BOOK OF THE
ZODIAC

THE LITTLE BOOK OF THE ZODIAC

An Hachette UK Company
www.hachette.co.uk

Summersdale Publishers Ltd
Part of Octopus Publishing Group Limited
Carmelite House
50 Victoria Embankment
LONDON
EC4Y 0DZ
UK

www.summersdale.com

Printed and bound in China

ISBN: 978-1-78685-546-6

Substantial discounts on bulk quantities of Summersdale books are available to corporations, professional associations and other organisations. For details contact general enquiries: telephone: +44 (0) 1243 771107 or email: enquiries@summersdale.com.

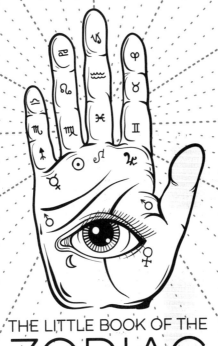

THE LITTLE BOOK OF THE
ZODIAC

MARION WILLIAMSON

summersdale

CONTENTS

THERE IS NO BETTER BOAT THAN A HOROSCOPE TO HELP A MAN CROSS OVER THE SEA OF LIFE.

VARĀHAMIHIRA

INTRODUCTION

You are at the start of a voyage of self-discovery that gets more fascinating the more you learn. Astrology is an extraordinarily rich subject as vast and mysterious as the night sky. So where do you start? You begin with the most important object in our solar system – the Sun. We open by looking at how the Sun's position in the sky at your birth relates to the horoscopes you read in a newspaper, then work our way through each of the planets examining their magical influences on your character and your future. This little book may be for beginners but by its end you'll have all the tools you'll need to make your own revealing discoveries into what makes you, and the people around you, tick.

PART 1

WHAT IS ASTROLOGY?

There is so much more to astrology than the columns you read in magazines and newspapers. Astrology is an all-encompassing study of human experience. It offers profound insight into our personal motivation and behaviour as well as helping us understand our relationships with others. Astrology teaches us that everything is part of an interconnected reality. Understanding how the ancient symbolism of the stars and planets can relate to events in your own life is a constantly evolving process. Astrology is a mirror of our world in the heavens, a search for human meaning in the skies. When modern science discovered that the galaxies in the cosmos and the microbes in the earth were all made of atoms, we recognised the truth in the ancient adage, 'As above, so below' – in other words, we are all made of stars!

WHAT ASTROLOGY CAN DO FOR YOU

Astrology doesn't predict your future or describe your personality in certain terms; instead it describes the potential for particular characteristics or events to come to light. Astrology can help you know what you are capable of as a human being, and when to take advantage of challenging or opportunistic times. Astrology does not negate your own free will – you are not controlled by the planets – but the planets do create certain atmospheres and conditions that you can learn to use to your advantage.

AN INSIGHT INTO YOUR PERSONALITY

When you understand why you act in a certain way or acknowledge your fears or desires, you feel more at ease with yourself and your world. When you know yourself better you act with conscious awareness of what you're doing and why. Your birth chart (also known as a natal chart or horoscope) is a diagram that shows the planets' exact positions at the moment of your birth. Studying your birth chart can reveal skills or talents that you ignore because they are so natural to you. You can find out what kind of career would be most fulfilling or indeed what kind of job would bore you to tears. Through studying your own chart you'll learn about your own motivation – your beliefs, desires and real needs – rather than trying on different guises and wondering why things don't work out. You'll discover what you need from a relationship, or what habits you fall into after you've been together a long time. Your attitude to money is shown in your horoscope as are the sort of situations where you're likely to gain or lose it. The better you understand your birth chart, the more whole you'll feel as a person.

HOW ASTROLOGY BEGAN

Astrology was born when the first humans gazed at the sky in wonder. The life-giving force of the Sun's vital energy was worshipped as the ultimate creator and the Moon's mysterious cycles were carefully observed for their effect on rivers and tides. The oldest lunar calendars date back to 32,000 BC and this fascinating art still continues to inspire us today.

DIFFERENT ASTROLOGICAL APPLICATIONS AND TECHNIQUES

There are as many types of astrology as there are ways to use it and they evolve and change in different ways. Here are just some of the most widely practised.

PSYCHOLOGICAL OR MODERN ASTROLOGY

This is the most popular type of astrology practised in the West today and the focus of what shall be covered in this book. Alan Leo propelled astrology back into the limelight in the late 1800s and early 1900s by suggesting it could be used to describe people's personalities and motivations. He moved astrology away from fortune telling, helping it evolve into a method of exploring character from a psychological perspective. Carl Jung, the founder of analytical psychology, recognised astrology as a form of 'synchronicity' or 'meaningful coincidence'. Where Freud assumed that people develop character from birth onwards, Jung declared that our character and personality is innate – something we are born with. Jungian astrologer Liz Greene describes the birth chart as a 'Map of the Psyche' and says that with its help we will come to a better understanding of our true nature.

HORARY

In Horary astrology the astrologer tries to answer a question by creating a horoscope for the exact time the question is asked and understood by the astrologer. Depending on the methods used, the answer could be complex or a straight 'yes' or 'no'.

MUNDANE

Mundane astrology is the study of the planets' effects on groups of people or countries. Birth charts can be drawn up for any moment in time. Mundane astrologers are particularly interested in moments in history when a significant event occurs. This could be the 'birth' of a new nation or country (such as the formation of the United Kingdom on 1 May 1707), a newly inaugurated president, an attack such as the one carried out on the World Trade Centre, a declaration of war or even an earthquake. A horoscope can be created for any event to see how people will cope and react to any changing circumstances.

ELECTIVE

Elective astrology is where an astrologer decides the best time for something to occur, based on the favourable

13

conditions of the planets. For example, if you wanted to know the best date to get married, an elective astrologer would look at your birth chart and base the date of the wedding on when Venus (the planet of love and harmony) would be in an auspicious condition in the sky when compared with Venus's position in your own birth chart.

RELATIONSHIP

Relationship astrology is where two or more birth charts are compared to see how people get along. There are two popular methods – synastry, where the two separate birth charts are compared to each other, and composite, which calculates the midpoints of each person's planets to form one chart. Midpoints are the halfway points in the 12 signs of the zodiac between your planets and your partner's. For example, if your Sun is in Taurus and your partner's Sun is in Cancer the midpoint would be taken as Gemini. Or if your Moon was in Leo and your partner's was in Sagittarius your midpoint would be somewhere in Libra. The chart takes each planet's midpoint to create one separate chart to be interpreted.

TRADITIONAL

Where modern psychological astrology focuses on explanation, traditional astrology concentrates on prediction and only uses the seven planets you can see with the naked eye (up to and including Saturn). Up until the twentieth century, almost all types of astrology were 'traditional'.

LOCATIONAL ASTROLOGY

This technique uses the time of birth to calculate ideal or compatible places or zones around the globe that work best with the person's own personal planets. If you wish to know the best places to enjoy a holiday the locational astrologer would be able to tell you where Venus (enjoyment) and Jupiter (long distance travel) would give you the greatest chance of a delightful trip. Different planets and techniques are used to suggest the most auspicious places to work, live or get married abroad. It's also known as astro-mapping.

MEDICAL ASTROLOGY

This ancient astrological technique, also known as iatromathematics, uses the person's birth chart to determine where or what may cause health problems. Each area of the body, the disease itself and the cures, all pertain to specific planetary correspondences.

DIFFERENT ASTROLOGICAL TRADITIONS

Different cultures around the globe have developed their own astrological traditions and systems.

WESTERN

The psychological system most commonly used in the West is a continuation of an ancient form of astrology based on the 12 signs of the zodiac. In Western popular culture this type of astrology is often condensed down to the Sun sign horoscopes focusing on the characteristics of the 12 constellations.

CHINESE

This system uses Chinese philosophy, yin and yang and is based on Chinese lunar cycles and five elemental types: Wood, Fire, Earth, Metal and Water. Each year is associated with an animal and element.

VEDIC

Vedic astrology, also known as Jyotish, is one of the oldest and most popular Eastern astrological traditions. The system uses the sidereal zodiac – the fixed, observable positions of the constellations, as we see them in the sky. This is different from the tropical zodiac used in Western astrology that is based on the relative and changeable position of the Sun. Jyotish also uses an additional Moon-based zodiac that divides the sky into 28 'lunar mansions'.

MAYAN

The Mayan astrological tradition is practised mainly in the West and South America and uses the ancient and complex calendar system known as the Tzolk'in and consists of 20 day signs and 13 galactic numbers, making a 260-day calendar 'year'. The Tzolk'in can be used to determine what will happen at particular times or for identifying personality types. Mayan astrology doesn't use elements but looks at directions, north, east, south, west, and each of the 20 day signs are assigned with a direction, each with its own set of meanings.

TRANSITS – PREDICTING OPPORTUNITIES OR CHALLENGES

Your birth chart is a snapshot of the planets' exact positions at your birth, which gives you a tremendous amount of insight into your personality. But the moment after that picture was taken the planets changed their positions. Astrologers describe these moving planets as 'transiting' and their movements give astrologers information about your future. Transits can highlight opportunities to be taken advantage of or challenges to be aware of. Most practised astrologers will be familiar with the planets' current positions but you can easily find out by looking up the current date in a book called a planetary ephemeris or discover this information online.

A PHYSICIAN WITHOUT A KNOWLEDGE OF ASTROLOGY HAS NO RIGHT TO CALL HIMSELF A PHYSICIAN.

HIPPOCRATES

THE SIGNS OF THE ZODIAC

The Sun, Moon and planets travel on a set path through the sky known as the ecliptic.

The 12 constellations that these bodies pass through are known as signs of the zodiac. Or at least that's the easiest way to look at it. In fact, the actual constellations and the signs of the zodiac associated with them are different. This is because the 'real' constellations are of different sizes and widths. In astrology all the signs are of equal length – 30 degrees – to enable the 12 signs to form a perfect 360-degree circle. The word 'zodiac' comes from ancient Greek and means 'circle of animals' and most of the constellations of the zodiac are named after animals: The Ram, The Bull, The Crab, and so on. Most of these names date to Babylonian times and before, and were based on the shape of the groups of stars, and at what time of year they were most visible.

ELEMENTAL TYPES

Each Sun sign belongs to one of four elemental types: Fire, Earth, Air and Water.

Fire signs

Aries, Leo, Sagittarius
Fire signs are enthusiastic,
spontaneous, active and quick

Earth signs

Taurus, Virgo, Capricorn
Earth signs are practical, stable,
determined and cautious

Air signs

Gemini, Libra, Aquarius
Air signs are intellectual, outgoing,
idealistic and versatile

Water signs

Cancer, Scorpio, Pisces
Water signs are intuitive, imaginative,
empathic and sensitive

THE CELESTIAL BODY

Each Sun sign corresponds with a particular area of the body starting at the head with the first sign Aries, and ending at the feet with the last sign, Pisces.

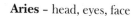

Aries – head, eyes, face

Taurus – neck, throat, ears

Gemini – hands, arms, nervous system

Cancer – breasts, stomach, womb

Leo – heart, upper back, spine

Virgo – large and small intestines, pancreas

Libra – lower back, kidneys, adrenals

Scorpio – genitals, bladder, urinary tract

Sagittarius – liver, hips, thighs

Capricorn – knees, bones, teeth

Aquarius – ankles, calves, shins

Pisces – feet, immune system

PART 2

YOUR SUN SIGN CHARACTER

Earth makes one revolution of the Sun each year and, by doing so, the Sun spends approximately one month in each of the 12 zodiac signs. The sign that the Sun was transiting at the time of your birth is known as your Sun sign. Astrology based upon your Sun sign is a generalised outline of your individual astrological characteristics. It is not possible to be a 'pure' Leo or Taurus. For that to happen all the other planets in your horoscope would have to be in Leo or Taurus, too, which because of their orbits and distances from each other, could never happen. But because the Sun is the most influential of the celestial objects in your horoscope, you can learn a great deal about yourself from this information alone. To gain a true and complete picture of your real character you must synthesise the Sun's influence with that of all the other planets in your horoscope. In the following three parts of this book you will discover the cosmic secrets of the three most important elements of your birth chart – your Sun, Rising and Moon sign.

ARIES - THE RAM

(21 March–20 April)

Aries people are brave, headstrong and beguilingly childish. But they can also be impatient, impulsive and restless. They love an adventure and charge at any obstacles in their path. They have a vibrant energy and their enthusiasm is hard to resist. The Aries determination to succeed is legendary and makes them natural born leaders. Rams are independent creatures, and at work they like being the boss. Aries are passionate and fall in love easily. Their natural spontaneity and honesty make them easy to trust because they always wear their heart on their sleeve.

Best character trait: courage

Element: Fire

Ruling planet: Mars

General characteristics: assertive, spontaneous, impatient

Body part: head

Why is Aries the first sign of the zodiac?

It may seem strange that the zodiacal calendar begins in March, but the reason for this dates back to Ancient Rome, when March was the first month of the year. It was changed to January by Julius Caesar in 46 BC. Coincidentally, Aries is ruled by the planet Mars in astrology. Mars was the Roman god of war, and this is how the month of March got its name. Late March heralds the vernal equinox and the start of spring – a time for new beginnings.

TAURUS – THE BULL

(21 April-21 May)

Taureans are patient, dependable and persevering. Their quiet strength and determination inspires others to trust them and they are faithful to their friends and loved ones. Taureans are stubborn and not fond of change and they won't be rushed into hasty decisions. Their strongest desire is for personal security and a comfortable home life. Bulls don't give their hearts away easily. They can be slow to make their minds up about relationships. But once their mind is made up, they'll do everything in their power to make things work.

Best character trait: strength

Element: Earth

Ruling planet: Venus

General characteristics: loyal, possessive, patient

Body part: neck

GEMINI - THE TWINS

(22 May–21 June)

Geminis are curious, quick-witted and light-hearted. They're named after the twins Castor and Pollux in Greek mythology because they can display two very different sides to their personality – cheerful and upbeat one minute then seething and withdrawn the next. Geminis can juggle many projects simultaneously and easily adapt to new surroundings and circumstances. But they can be a little fickle. Geminis can be incurable flirts, with their romantic lives being as colourful as their taste in clothes. They have a natural gift for finding something in common with even the most difficult of people.

Best character trait: adaptable

Element: Air

Ruling planet: Mercury

General characteristics: curious, clever, quick

Body part: arms

CANCER - THE CRAB

(22 June–22 July)

Cancerians are tenacious, caring and immensely protective of the people they care about. Like the hard shell of the crab, they project a tougher exterior than they actually have, to hide their sensitive nature. When a tenacious Cancerian has what they want in their pincers, it's difficult to convince them to give it up, even if it's no longer useful to them. Cancerians are the hoarders of the zodiac and need to learn to let go and trust that everything will be OK, even if they're not in control.

Best character trait: caring

Element: Water

Ruling planet: the Moon

General characteristics: sensitive, emotional, tenacious

Body part: chest

LEO – THE LION

(23 July–22 August)

Ruled by the creative life-force of the Sun, Leos light up and energise the people around them. These proud, flamboyant people crave attention and feel diminished without an adoring audience. Creative and organised, a typical Leo can become a little bossy with the people they care about. Leos are more easily hurt than most people realise and even constructive criticism can be a blow to their ego. But when a Leo feels loved and trusted they will move mountains to please the people they care about.

Best character trait: generosity

Element: Fire

Ruling planet: the Sun

General characteristics: outgoing, popular, creative

Body part: heart

VIRGO – THE VIRGIN

(23 August–23 September)

Virgos are the busiest sign in the zodiac with an inexhaustible to-do list. If you want something done, ask a Virgo and if they can't manage it they'll know someone who can. Virgos are full of excellent advice but in their pursuit of perfection they can sometimes appear critical, when they're just trying to help you be the best you can be. In love Virgos are thoughtful, kind and patient though they need to learn to relax and let the small things take care of themselves.

Best character trait: organised

Element: Earth

Ruling planet: Mercury

General characteristics: capable, perfectionist, efficient

Body part: intestines

LIBRA – THE SCALES

(24 September–23 October)

Librans strive for harmony in all areas of their lives. They are not loners and learn their most important lessons from other people. If left to their own devices, these charming, diplomatic individuals can take an age to make any important decisions, so it's essential to them to find someone to bat ideas back and forth with, to help them understand themselves and their lives better. Relationships can be a tough testing ground as their expectations are high. Learning to enjoy their own company and their independence is Libra's greatest lesson.

Best character trait: fairness

Element: Air

Ruling planet: Venus

General characteristics: sociable, charming, easy-going

Body part: hips

SCORPIO – THE SCORPION

(24 October–22 November)

Scorpios draw from deep pools of emotional and physical energy and need to find a positive outlet for their intense feelings. At work Scorpios push themselves and enjoy a challenge – the more daunting the better. Power games can arise if jealousies are stirred, and that's when the legendary Scorpio 'stinger' is most likely to make an appearance. But if you have a Scorpio's trust you'll have a deeply intuitive and loyal partner or friend. What would benefit Scorpio most is to let down their defences and accept that they too can be vulnerable.

Best character trait: willpower

Element: Water

Ruling planet: Pluto

General characteristics: intense, penetrating, resourceful

Body part: sex organs

SAGITTARIUS – THE ARCHER

(23 November–21 December)

Sagittarians are freedom-loving spirits who thrive on challenge and adventure. Ruled by optimistic Jupiter, Sagittarius has an infectiously enthusiastic approach to life and can become bored when expected to respect customs and stick to rules and regulations. Because of their fear of being stifled or restricted, a typical Sagittarian needs a broadminded, inspiring partner who will understand their innate restlessness and try to keep their relationship fresh and exciting. Sagittarius needs to learn that the grass is not always greener on the other side of the fence.

Best character trait: enthusiastic

Element: Fire

Ruling planet: Jupiter

General characteristics: adventurous, broadminded, optimistic

Body part: thighs

CAPRICORN – THE GOAT

(22 December–20 January)

Patient, determined and always realistic, Capricorn people don't rush into anything. They have a cool, logical approach to any situation and work out a careful plan to achieve their aims. They're not flashy, loud or boastful but they are winners. Underneath that composed exterior is a loyal, devoted partner who will try to move mountains for the right person. Capricorns also have a wicked sense of humour and would do well to remember that happiness and worldly success are not always the same thing.

Best character trait: determination

Element: Earth

Ruling planet: Saturn

General characteristics: reserved, realistic, ambitious

Body part: knees

AQUARIUS – THE WATER CARRIER

(21 January–19 February)

Eccentric, inventive Aquarian people can come across as a little bit 'out there' or ahead of their time. Humanitarian and friendly to a fault, Aquarians feel at home with many varied groups of people. Their insatiable curiosity about others is one of their most endearing qualities but it can be difficult for them to relate to people on a deeper, more emotional level. To be happy in love they need a partner that appreciates their need for independence and can give them space to grow.

Best character trait: ingenuity

Element: Air

Ruling planet: Uranus

General characteristics: eccentric, independent, original

Body part: ankles

PISCES - THE FISH

(20 February–20 March)

Piscean people are gentle, compassionate and understanding. The Piscean symbol of two fish swimming in the opposite direction sums up much of the Piscean dual nature. Pisceans may know what they ought to do but quite often they get sucked along by the line of least resistance. Pisces are romantic, poetic partners who excel at expressing their innermost feelings to the people they love. Pisceans need to learn that when they ignore difficult situations they might have to deal with even more confusing consequences later on.

Best character trait: empathy

Element: Water

Ruling planet: Neptune

General characteristics: dreamy, psychic, gentle

Body part: feet

OPHIUCHUS – THE THIRTEENTH SIGN?

From time to time the idea that there should
be a thirteenth sign of the zodiac raises its head.
The argument being that because of the Earth's
tilt/wobble its position has changed from that
of 3,000 years ago when the signs were first
allocated, and the Sun now appears to pass
through 13 signs instead of 12. But astrology is
not astronomy. Astrology focuses on the patterns
of the planets and the Moon as they pass through
12 zones defined by the relationship between
the Earth and Sun. Those zones have the same
names as constellations, but they are not the
same as the actual constellations. Western
astrology uses the tropical zodiac that follows the
seasons, based on the position of the Sun's rays
and the tropics. Ophiuchus is a constellation but
the Sun does not pass through the constellation
because it sits just outside of the ecliptic (the path
of the Sun through the sky). There are more than
20 constellations that touch or border the ecliptic
but in Western astrology only 12 are used.

PART 3

YOUR SUN SIGN IS JUST THE BEGINNING

Your personal birth chart is a blend of different types of planetary energy, and for a much more detailed and insightful look into your character you must look beyond your Sun sign. You also have a Rising sign, a Moon sign, a Mercury sign, a Venus sign and so on through the different planets. It is this information that is used by astrologers to create your personalised birth chart. To find out exactly where each of the planets were when you were born, you'll need to look up your birthday in a planetary ephemeris – a book that shows which planets were in which sign, which sign and phase the Moon was in, as well as other information such as the direction the planets were travelling at the time. Before there were computer programmes to help you create your birth chart, all this information was calculated by hand, using an ephemeris. Luckily now there are websites that do all the hard work for you.

RISING SIGNS

WHAT IS A RISING SIGN?

Your Rising sign, also known as your Ascendant, was the constellation that was rising (ascending) on the eastern horizon at the time of your birth. It is relatively easy to find this information out online (see page 122 for recommendations) but in the past astrologers worked it out by hand. Each zodiac sign takes approximately two hours to rise over the Ascendant. That's all 12 signs of the zodiac in a 24-hour period – one day. Your Rising sign is essential for an accurate birth chart – and this is why astrologers can be so pushy for you to give them as exact a time of birth as possible. Twins born five minutes apart would very likely share the same Sun sign but each could have a different Rising sign, which could make their birth charts – and therefore their personalities – quite different.

WHY IS YOUR RISING SIGN IMPORTANT?

If your Sun sign is your core personality, your Rising sign is your own self-image, or the personality you choose to present to the world. Usually when you meet someone at a party you first encounter their

Rising sign because that's the side of their personality they're most comfortable to project. As you get to know someone better, you peel back layers - starting from the outer shell of the Rising sign, through to the 'core' characteristics of your Sun sign (who you really are) through to your emotional centre - your Moon sign - and so on through each planetary layer. Your Rising sign is the filter through which your personality is expressed; the first impression you give to others and the mask you choose to wear. Your Rising sign is your default position and describes how you deal with life's challenges. Most people identify more strongly with their Rising sign than they do with their Sun sign.

YOUR RISING SIGN CHARACTER

ARIES RISING

The default position for an Aries Rising person is to act. Their instincts are to tackle things head on, even if they are not entirely sure how that's going to work out yet. Aries Rising wants to be first in the queue and has a fiercely independent streak. Act now and think later has probably led to some awkward situations in the past but their courage and disarmingly candid approach usually means they get exactly what they set their hearts on.

TAURUS RISING

Individuals with Taurus Rising have a quiet, serene way about them. They don't do anything in a hurry. When problems occur they wait, chew things over and let it percolate. Taurus Risers are sensitive to disharmony. Clashing colours, noise and irritable people make them feel uncomfortable and they'll avoid conflict if they can. Their homes are peaceful, cosy and tasteful. If there are soft cushions, a cup of tea and biscuits on the go, you're probably inside a Taurus Riser's house. Taurus Rising people are often artistic, musical or have lovely singing voices.

GEMINI RISING

Gemini Risers react to any new people or situations by talking at them. Who? What? When? Where? They deal with the world by trying to measure, weigh, categorise or learn from it. Gemini Risers are very adaptable and often deal with any problems life throws at them by initiating changes. This can bring new life and ideas into stagnant situations along with some much-needed humour. Gemini Ascendant types are usually good-natured and friendly but sometimes they miss what's going on under the surface with people, because they're so busy talking. But because of their endless curiosity they are excellent at encouraging others to talk and are skilled negotiators.

CANCER RISING

Cancer Rising individuals aren't always comfortable in new environments with people they don't know. They tend to creep back into their shell where they feel safe and slowly gain energy as they feel more courage. When faced with a problem, they hold back from offering a solution until they have thought about it alone. Cancer Rising types are rarely aggressive, but if they feel that the people they love or their home is being threatened, they will defend their ground passionately. Sensitive souls at heart, Cancer Risers enjoy looking after other people. Close friends often feel that they are part of the family.

LEO RISING

Leo Risers are born entertainers and are proud of their creative skills. They like to be the centre of attention, but their generosity and warmth makes people forgive their slightly inflated egos. When faced with new people or circumstances, Leo Rising's natural instincts are to take control of the situation. They have excellent organisational skills, which can at times come across as pushy. But for all their bossiness Leo Risers hate to be thought of badly. They're people pleasers at heart and they need to be admired and approved of. Leo Rising people need to form a good opinion of themselves before seeking it elsewhere.

VIRGO RISING

Virgo Rising people are kind-hearted and like to be of practical use to others. They have a knack for knowing what to do to make people feel better and are skilled in turning chaos into workable situations. When faced with any challenges, Virgo Rising's instincts are to find the simplest, most elegant solution. Kind and understanding, Virgo Risers help others to heal and they would benefit from a little of their own compassionate self-analysis to work out some of their own issues.

LIBRA RISING

When you first meet a Libra Rising person they'll come across as charming, well-mannered and sociable. These diplomatic types are naturally sociable and want to make people feel at ease in their company. Libra Rising characters deal with life's ups and downs by working out what the fairest course of action would be – even if sometimes it takes them an awfully long time to make up their minds. Libra Rising types spend much of their time making their environment, and their own appearances, as pleasant as possible. Libra Ascendant people can be a little passive, too keen to adapt to everyone else's idea of who they should be, rather than having confidence in who they actually are.

SCORPIO RISING

Scorpio Rising individuals have passion and intensity pouring out of every pore. They're strong-willed and deal with life's challenges by getting to the truth of what's really going on. Insightful and unflinching, people with a Scorpio Ascendant are not frightened by strong emotions – they're fuelled by them. These characters go to enormous lengths to protect their own true feelings, fearing if their true hearts are discovered it would weaken them and lay them open to manipulation. But when they let their guard down they're loyal, fiercely protective of the people they love and capable of immense emotional courage. Scorpio Rising people sometimes spend too long navel gazing when the truth can be right in front of their face.

SAGITTARIUS RISING

Sagittarius Rising types are boisterous, exuberant and larger-than-life. They treat life's challenges as a game and their happy-go-lucky attitude means they usually come out winning. They enjoy competition and sport and have a need for frequent changes of scenery. They can become very restless if life becomes too predictable or if they have too many responsibilities. Sagittarius Rising types don't often need the same home comforts that the other signs require and can be as happy sleeping in a hammock as they would in a more salubrious environment. A Sagittarius Ascendant gives individuals real optimism and an ability to inspire others to make their dreams a reality. Sagittarius Rising characters can be a little tactless and need to develop a more subtle attitude to people who are of a more sensitive disposition.

CAPRICORN RISING

There's a certain shyness to a Capricorn Rising individual that's at odds with their enormous capacity to succeed. These individuals have a practical outlook when faced with new or challenging situations and their eminently sensible advice is usually wise beyond their years. They might not be the first person to pipe up when asked for their opinion, but when encouraged, these characters will come up with a brilliant plan – albeit a little too realistic and gritty for many people's tastes. Capricorn Rising doesn't like to give anyone false hope but perhaps they could work on selling themselves with a little more pizzazz.

AQUARIUS RISING

A typical Aquarius Rising person will usually think or act differently to most other people. They deal with life's challenges and new situations by looking for unique solutions or by taking a completely independent view. Unconventional by nature, Aquarius Rising can find it natural to rebel against social norms and they are often keen supporters of those involved in social or political injustice. Aquarian Rising people are often at the forefront of social change. The desire to think so differently from the crowd can sometimes make others feel a little alienated from the Aquarian Rising person. These unique characters would do well to remember it is what they have in common with others that creates bonds, not what they do differently.

PISCES RISING

A typical Pisces Rising person has a gentle, if slightly vague way about them. They rarely kick up a fuss and usually dislike being in the limelight. Their moods change rapidly and their reaction to change or life's challenges is usually to hide until the unsettling situation has passed. Pisces Rising people can find it tricky to focus their energies on one thing, preferring to have many half-finished projects to revisit when they feel like it. Pisces Rising people would benefit from the occasional reality check – just to make sure they're swimming in the right direction.

PART 4

MOON SIGNS

Your Moon sign refers to the astrological sign the Moon was travelling through at the time you were born. The Moon takes two and a half days to travel through each sign of the zodiac – roughly one month to make a complete cycle. The Moon's changeable, reflective nature mirrors our own instinctual and emotional responses through its different phases and conditions. Understanding your Moon sign is vitally important because it provides the key to your emotional nature. You can find your Moon sign from looking up your date of birth in a planetary ephemeris, or by looking it up online (see recommendations on page 122).

YOUR MOON SIGN CHARACTER

MOON IN ARIES

As the first sign of the zodiac, Aries Moon sign people can be a little self-centred, focusing first on their own needs before working out how others will be affected. Moon in Aries people are impulsive and are fast to feel love or anger. Their emotional reactions are lightning-fast, ardent and decisive and because they feel so strongly, so quickly, they don't often have the time to think through the consequences of their actions. Aries Moon people are honest and straightforward and perhaps a little 'on the nose' at times, with their loved ones preferring a less thoughtless approach. But when Moon in Aries people feel passionate about someone or something they give it every ounce of their passion. They have learned from character-forming mistakes to hold back on their first impulses – but this is a life-long project.

Aries Moon's lesson: Moon in Aries individuals should try to learn to temper their fight or flight responses and let a feeling settle before feeling the need to take action.

MOON IN TAURUS

Moon in Taurus people need to feel secure. They're generally calm, serene people whose immediate reactions tend to be slow. But once they have made up their mind about something or someone it's almost impossible to convince them to change their opinion. These patient people don't rush headlong into anything. They're careful planners who take other people's feelings seriously and they like to follow a conventional path when it comes to courting, generally agreeing that a traditional approach to love is the right path. Taurus Moon characters are usually very even tempered but a slow build-up of resentment over months or even years can lead to an explosive, destructive outburst.

Taurus Moon's lesson: Taurus Moons should try to trust their first instincts and get in touch with their childish spontaneity rather than waiting too long to decide how they feel.

MOON IN GEMINI

A Gemini Moon person has quick, witty responses and a light-hearted approach to their own emotions. They tend to draw from their own logic and experience rather than using their instincts when it comes to understanding others on an emotional level, which can give them an air of superficiality. A Gemini Moon person usually has a questioning, intellectual approach when dealing with other people's feelings, which helps identify what's really going on without getting too emotionally involved.

Gemini Moon's lesson: Gemini Moon people need to learn that the people they are most attracted to physically may not be who they are most compatible with emotionally.

MOON IN CANCER

Each zodiac sign is associated with a planet and Cancer's planetary ruler is the Moon. People with a Cancer Moon are generally very comfortable with their feelings. The reactions of Moon in Cancer people are defensive, protective and deeply instinctual. Cancerian Moons have legendary intuition. They feel responsible for others' emotional wellbeing and have a strong need to nurture the people closest to them. A comfortable home life and tight family connections are top priorities for these intuitive, caring individuals. Cancerian Moon sign types are tenacious. When they know what or whom they want they can fixate on that one goal and it can be difficult for Crabs to remove their pincers from something once they get stuck in.

Cancer Moon's lesson: Cancerian Moons need to learn that their emotional needs will change – that what they wanted ten years ago may be completely different today.

MOON IN LEO

Leo's immediate emotional response is to take control, often in a rather melodramatic manner. They like to be at the centre of what's going on, and have been known to create emotional dramas just to raise the excitement levels up a few notches. Leo Moon types have a load of love to give, but without this affection mirrored back to them they curl up like a dead leaf. But when they feel their love is reciprocated these big-hearted souls light up like a Christmas tree and spread their warmth and good humour into even the darkest shadows.

Leo Moon's lesson: Leo Moons need to learn that if they are going to dish out advice, they also have to learn what it feels like to take it.

MOON IN VIRGO

Moon in Virgo people are quite timid emotionally, hoping they can work out their feelings in a logical, ordered way. Moon in Virgo types love to feel appreciated and needed and they show their affection for those they love by helping them in many small ways. Although they are affectionate they can be a little bit stiff in expressing themselves in an intimate way and if they feel stressed or unhappy they can become sceptical, overly fussy and critical. When Moon in Virgo people really like someone they're usually shy to admit their feelings initially. But when they feel more secure they open up and share a romantic, poetic side of themselves that is rarely seen by others.

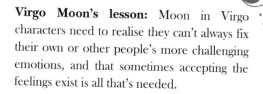

Virgo Moon's lesson: Moon in Virgo characters need to realise they can't always fix their own or other people's more challenging emotions, and that sometimes accepting the feelings exist is all that's needed.

MOON IN LIBRA

Moon in Libra characters need people around them to help them understand the world they live in. Their emotional responses rely heavily on what the people closest to them think and feel, and they often adopt others' stronger opinions as a basis for their own. Libra Moon people hate confrontation and are very sensitive to discord or upset – that's what makes them excellent negotiators and peacekeepers. Harmony must be restored at all costs, but sometimes that price means a little too much self-sacrifice or belief that others' feelings are more important than their own.

Libra Moon's lesson: Libra Moon people need to learn that being alone isn't a scary place to be.

MOON IN SCORPIO

Moon in Scorpio people have an emotional life that can seem very different to the side of their personality that they choose to show the world. Scorpio Moons have very deep, powerful feelings that they are usually trying their best to keep hidden from others. They have a fear of being laid bare in case they're taken advantage of in some way and trust isn't always easy. But when they feel safe and loved Scorpio Moon types will do anything in their considerable power to pay back the loyalty and love that's given to them in good faith.

Scorpio Moon's lesson: Scorpio Moon people heal by exposing their pain to the world instead of always trying to keep it hidden or disguised.

MOON IN SAGITTARIUS

A typical Sagittarius Moon person's responses are open, honest and enthusiastic. They don't tend to dwell on their emotions for too long, believing that action speaks far louder than feelings or words. As a freedom-loving Fire sign these characters don't like to feel tied down, especially when younger. They can get a little claustrophobic emotionally but are warm, philosophical and generous to a fault when they feel appreciated. Sagittarius Moon people aren't sentimental but should try not to be too tactless when dealing with other people's feelings.

Sagittarius Moon's lesson: Sagittarius Moon types must learn to deal with the situation in front of them rather than running away from it, because the same thing will crop up again and again until dealt with properly.

MOON IN CAPRICORN

Capricorn Moon people can appear very cool emotionally, even a little reserved or remote. Their initial emotional responses can be a little on the negative side but there is always a strong urge to be productive and practical. Not natural risk-takers, Capricorn Moon types weigh up the pros and cons before committing themselves to a particular person, but when they do it's usually with total faith that the partnership will be a success. They take their duties very seriously and don't mess with people's hearts lightly.

Capricorn Moon's lesson: Capricorn Moons need to learn that opening up to others about their insecurities or fears can be a healing experience.

MOON IN AQUARIUS

Moon in Aquarius people are intriguing, charismatic individuals who tend to intellectualise their feelings rather than giving over to them. They rarely judge others and are more likely to be able to accept, or even prefer, an unconventional relationship of some sort. Warmth and passion might not be so obvious with a Moon in Aquarius person on a one-to-one basis but there is a genuine humanitarian wish to make the world a better place for everyone.

Aquarian Moon's lesson: the lesson for Moon in Aquarius people is that sharing on an emotional level will help give them the feeling of connectedness with others they crave.

MOON IN PISCES

Sensitive souls, Moon in Pisces people react to life's challenges and surprises by tuning into other people's feelings and emotions. They are so empathic that sometimes it's difficult to distinguish their own feelings from those of the people around them. It's very important that the people closest to them have their best interests at heart otherwise they can absorb negative energies, or become pulled in two directions. If a Piscean Moon person is unhappy they can escape into unhealthy habits when the best outlet for their feelings is to be creative and express their feelings through music, art, poetry and writing.

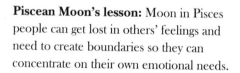

Piscean Moon's lesson: Moon in Pisces people can get lost in others' feelings and need to create boundaries so they can concentrate on their own emotional needs.

WE ARE BORN AT A GIVEN
MOMENT, IN A GIVEN PLACE AND,
LIKE VINTAGE YEARS OF WINE,
WE HAVE THE QUALITIES OF
THE YEAR AND OF THE SEASON
OF WHICH WE ARE BORN.

CARL JUNG

PART 5

THE PLANETS

We have covered the Sun's vital importance in describing the basic personality and how the Moon's sign colours the emotions. Then when we combine these with the Rising sign's traits we're starting to form a picture of the whole personality. But of course people are complex and unique and so is their astrology. The next step is to take a look at the individual planets and their meanings, then to synthesise these to give an even richer portrait of what's going on with an individual's horoscope. Every planet has its own set of keywords – words and phrases that describe its astrological meaning and purpose. Each planet affects a different part of your personality depending on the sign of the zodiac it was in, whether it was retrograde (appeared to be going backwards through the sky when you were born) and what angles it made to the other planets in your birth chart. These relationships are known as 'aspects'.

To find the position and sign that any planet occupied at your birth you can look them up in a planetary ephemeris or find them online at one of the recommended websites on page 122.

THE PLANETS AND THEIR MEANINGS

MERCURY AND VENUS'S ORBITS

Mercury and Venus both have orbits nearer the Sun than the Earth, so their positions in the zodiac are always in signs near to the Sun. For instance, if you have the Sun in Cancer, your Venus can only be in two signs before or after. And if your Mercury sign was Cancer it's even closer to the sun – so your Mercury sign could only be in the sign immediately before the sign the Sun was in (Gemini), the same as the Sun (Cancer) or the one right after (Leo).

 ## MERCURY – THE COMMUNICATIONS PLANET

In Greek mythology Hermes was known as the Messenger of the Gods, who was later named Mercury by the Romans. In astrology Mercury is the planet of communication and day-to-day expression. In the birth chart Mercury represents the mind – how we think, the way we speak and the kind of vocabulary we use. It rules our memory and thought processes and describes whether we are methodical thinkers or creative geniuses. Mercury shows how you draw conclusions, and its aspects and angles to other planets describe whether we are positive or negative, lazy or deep thinkers. Mercury's position in your birth chart indicates whether you like bouncing ideas off other people or prefer to work alone.

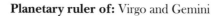

Planetary ruler of: Virgo and Gemini

Mercury keywords: thought, speech, interaction, memory, expression, dexterity, commerce

MERCURY RETROGRADE

The planet Mercury has influence on all types of communication, travel and negotiation. Three or four times a year it appears to stop (station) and then moves backward (retrograde) through the sky. This is actually an optical illusion caused by Mercury passing the Earth in its orbit – much like two trains passing each other, it creates the optical illusion that one (Mercury, in this case) is going backward. At these times the areas of life ruled by Mercury can appear to go haywire.

Phones stop working, emails go to the wrong person, conversations seem full of misunderstandings and details or small print can get the better of you. Travel plans get complicated and delays become more likely. Astrologically it's not the luckiest time to make large purchases or to hold a conference and computers should always be backed up!

MAKING THE MOST OF MERCURY RETROGRADE

Although traditionally not the best times to communicate with other people or to travel, Mercury retrograde weeks do offer a 'time out' period for self-reflection. These are the best points in the year to learn more about oneself because the information coming from the outside world could be misleading. Mercury retrograde teaches us that it's only what we want or feel that really matters in the end. It gives us the opportunity to make sure we are communicating clearly with ourselves – and helps us project our hopes and wishes back into the outside world in an effective way.

You can find out when Mercury is in retrograde by visiting one of the recommended websites (in the back of the book) or by looking up the dates in a planetary ephemeris.

MERCURY IN THE BIRTH CHART

Mercury in Fire signs (Aries, Leo, Sagittarius):

Fire sign Mercury people have sudden bursts of ideas and inspiration. They think on their feet, make quick decisions and back up their thoughts with quick action.

Mercury in Earth signs (Taurus, Virgo, Capricorn):

Earth sign Mercury types are deliberate, cautious thinkers who like to plan and organise their thoughts. They are the list makers of the zodiac.

Mercury in Air signs (Gemini, Libra, Aquarius):

Air sign Mercury types are intellectual, curious and quick-witted. They learn quickly, are good with languages and change their minds as quickly as they make them.

Mercury in Water signs (Cancer, Scorpio, Pisces):

Mercury Water signs are intuitive, insightful and fluid. They have good memories and can see past what's been said to what's actually meant.

VENUS – THE RELATIONSHIP PLANET

Venus describes what we value in life – and what we most enjoy doing. The planet of love and harmony describes our relationships with other people; how, what and who we love. Venus represents how we spend or save our money, whether we hang on to it or give it away freely. Through Venus we learn about what gives us pleasure, our skills and talents and what makes us happy. Venus's position in our horoscope also shows what or who we are attracted to, our sexuality and the way we express our love for other people.

Planetary ruler of: Taurus and Libra

Venus keywords: relationship, money, enjoyment, love, romance, art, harmony, charm, indulgence

VENUS IN THE BIRTH CHART

Venus in Fire signs (Aries, Leo, Sagittarius):

Fire sign Venus people love with passion and enthusiasm with a force to be reckoned with. They fall in love hard but move on quickly when things run out of steam.

Venus in Earth signs (Taurus, Virgo, Capricorn):

Earth sign Venus types are careful and thoughtful towards their partners. They are loyal and seek to build something stable, secure and enduring with the people they care about.

Venus in Air signs (Gemini, Libra, Aquarius):

Air sign Venus people have refined romantic tastes. It's important that they find their partners as stimulating mentally as they are physically.

Venus in Water signs (Cancer, Scorpio, Pisces):

Water sign Venus people love deeply and intensely. They long for a meaningful connection on an emotional level and searching for their true love can be an all-consuming desire.

MARS –
THE ACTION PLANET

Mars describes how we go about getting what we desire. Its position in the birth chart shows the type of drive, energy and enthusiasm at our disposal and the way we choose to direct our willpower. The sign our Mars occupies shows what kind of energy we put into changing things we're not happy with. It represents our willingness to compete and how we deal with winning or losing. Its position and sign expresses what we are compelled to fight for, how we express our own independence and how we stick up for ourselves.

Planetary ruler of: Aries

Mars keywords: action, assertion, selfishness, drive, energy, desire, direction, aggression, independence

MARS IN THE BIRTH CHART

Mars in Fire signs (Aries, Leo, Sagittarius):

Mars is happiest in the Fire signs where it feels naturally energised and powerful. Mars Fire sign types have natural reserves of willpower, energy and enthusiasm to help them reach their goals and make their mark on the world.

Mars in Earth signs (Taurus, Virgo, Capricorn):

Mars Earth signs assert themselves in a physical, material way by organising themselves and others to make, build or create something solid and worthwhile.

Mars in Air signs (Gemini, Libra, Aquarius):

When Mars is in an Air sign the individual's assertiveness is shown in an intellectual, idealistic way but with tremendous energy to see ideas through to their conclusion.

Mars in Water signs (Cancer, Scorpio, Pisces):

Mars in Water signs gives the individual tremendous emotional energy and insight. These are usually protective, emotionally wise souls who assert themselves with a subtle power.

 **JUPITER - THE OPPORTUNITY PLANET**

Jupiter is a lucky, joyful, expansive planet that describes our sense of belief and faith in ourselves and the world around us. Jupiter shows how we manifest luck and opportunity in our lives. Its position in the birth chart shows the skills and talents we naturally have and can expand on – how we find new opportunities and our capacity to learn. Jupiter represents our attitude to freedom and where we are most likely to meet with fortunate experiences or have a guardian angel helping us from behind the scenes.

Planetary ruler of: Sagittarius

Jupiter keywords: expansion, travel, philosophy, growth, faith, opportunity, excess, optimism, freedom, luck, abundance

JUPITER IN THE BIRTH CHART

Jupiter in Fire signs (Aries, Leo, Sagittarius):

Opportunities for Jupiter Fire sign people come when they take the initiative. These individuals make their own luck when they act on what they believe in.

Jupiter in Earth signs (Taurus, Virgo, Capricorn):

Earth Jupiter people have a philosophical attitude towards money and possessions. This is a 'guardian angel' influence, where resources often arrive out of the blue, exactly when they're needed.

Jupiter in Air signs (Gemini, Libra, Aquarius):

Jupiter Air signs' source of greatest growth and opportunity comes from their knack for bringing thoughts and ideas into the real world.

Jupiter in Water signs (Cancer, Scorpio, Pisces):

Jupiter in the Water signs gives these individuals faith in the power of their own emotions. When they trust their feelings and instincts, abundance flows through them.

SATURN – THE DISCIPLINE PLANET

Where Jupiter expands, Saturn contracts. Saturn shows where we experience discipline and control. Saturn describes which areas of life we need to work hardest at to become successful – where we learn tough but important lessons. This responsible planet describes where we can fulfil our destiny as well as showing where we have difficulties or feel inadequate. Facing karma isn't always easy. Saturn has a serious influence and a bearing on our sense of purpose and direction. This challenging planet also bestows the gift of time and teaches us where we need to do things properly. Saturn can be a hard taskmaster, but when we meet his stern gaze head on, the rewards are long-lasting and filled with an unshakable sense of true achievement.

Planetary ruler of: Capricorn

Saturn keywords: time, limitation, difficulty, lessons, karma, hard work, necessity, teachers, authority, achievement, fear

THE SATURN RETURN

Between every 28–29.5 years Saturn returns to the same position in the birth chart that it occupied at a person's birth. This is a cosmic rite of passage when we often feel anxiety or pressure put upon us to act like an adult. It can be a time of crisis when people realise they are headed in the wrong direction or that the life they are living isn't quite what they thought it would be. Often during a Saturn return is when we realise we have a lot of work to do before we can get where we want to be. Alternatively, Saturn can bring us extra responsibilities or promotions that we're more than happy about and we can be given a rare opportunity to prove ourselves to others. Usually by the second return when we are 56–60 we are able to review our life goals over the past 30 years and are offered a second chance to perfect them even further.

SATURN IN THE BIRTH CHART

Saturn in Fire signs (Aries, Leo, Sagittarius):

Saturn Fire people are discovering what it means to take the initiative and be self-sufficient. Exploring their considerable creative skills provides the key to their self-worth.

Saturn in Earth signs (Taurus, Virgo, Capricorn):

Saturn Earth people are learning the value of money and of taking responsibility for how they value or support themselves or use other people's resources. There may be a fear of losing security.

Saturn in Air signs (Gemini, Libra, Aquarius):

Saturn in Air signs experience a shyness or difficulty in expressing their thoughts or perhaps a fear of being ridiculed or not taken seriously.

Saturn in Water signs (Cancer, Scorpio, Pisces):

Saturn in Water people can feel frightened by the intensity of their own feelings. There can be some denial or repression to deal with or a reluctance to express their immediate instincts.

URANUS – THE REBELLIOUS PLANET

Uranus is the planet of change, rebellion and unexpected consequences. This changeable planet brings a new way of approaching life's problems through inventive, original or even unorthodox action. Its erratic, sometimes bizarre, influence stimulates us to try something new – or shows which parts of our own characters are unique, or where we refuse to bend to society's expectations of us. When people are in tune with Uranus's energies they can be true revolutionaries – extremely inspiring and enlightening with moments of life-changing genius.

Planetary ruler of: Aquarius

Uranus keywords: change, eccentric, unpredictable, erratic, inspirational, enlightening, rebellious, modern, community

URANUS IN THE BIRTH CHART

Uranus in Fire signs (Aries, Leo, Sagittarius):

Uranus Fire signs have independent, pioneering spirits and aren't frightened to be different. They're proud that they stand out from the crowd and often come up with unconventional solutions to their own problems and enjoy surprising people.

Uranus in Earth signs (Taurus, Virgo, Capricorn):

Uranus Earth people tend to take an unconventional approach to how they earn or spend their money and often have unusual jobs or eccentric lifestyles. They're interested in building a community spirit and enjoy sharing their resources for a more humanitarian existence.

Uranus in Air signs (Gemini, Libra, Aquarius):

Uranus is happiest in the Air signs where its unconventional and spirited energy is at home in the world of ideas and invention. Uranus in Air sign people often speak without thinking first, which can either be entertaining or annoying for others.

Uranus in Water signs (Cancer, Scorpio, Pisces):

Uranus Water people can be a little ill at ease with their emotional nature, preferring to try to rationalise any uncomfortable feelings with a logical approach. But if these characters don't take their emotions seriously enough, any unexpressed feelings will have a habit of rising to the surface in surprising ways.

 **NEPTUNE – THE IMAGINATIVE PLANET**

Neptune rules over the subconscious mind, spirituality, unseen forces and sensitivity. Hard to pin down, Neptune also represents the ability to deceive or be deceived, to believe or be deluded, to build illusions but also psychic perception, intuition and instinct. Neptune is the power of imagination, artistic abilities and empathy. The sea god's position in the birth chart shows where and what you give away and describes what ignites our compassion for others. It describes our dreams, our unconscious mind and our romantic illusions. Neptune's sign and position in the birth chart can reveal our metaphorical saviours – and tormentors.

Planetary ruler of: Pisces

Neptune keywords: psychic, mystical, deception, spiritual, compassion, charity, loss, confusion, romanticism, ideals

NEPTUNE IN THE BIRTH CHART

Neptune in Fire signs (Aries, Leo, Sagittarius):

Neptune Fire people are magnetic, glamorous but often difficult to get to know. They always keep people guessing but they're often a mystery to themselves, too.

Neptune in Earth signs (Taurus, Virgo, Capricorn):

Neptune Earth people can be impractical or evasive about money and possessions and sometimes they find it hard to hold on to what they own.

Neptune in Air signs (Gemini, Libra, Aquarius):

In Air signs Neptune encourages the imaginary and visionary abilities of people with this placement. But it can also emphasise escapist fantasies or unrealistic ideas.

Neptune in Water signs (Cancer, Scorpio, Pisces):

Water is Neptune's own element so the planet feels comfortable here. Neptune emphasises the emotional, intuitive abilities of those with this placement but can also encourage detachment or denial.

PLUTO – THE TRANSFORMATIONAL PLANET

Pluto was discovered in 1930 and, because it moves so slowly through the zodiac signs, is known as a 'generational' planet. Since its discovery it has only moved through seven signs of the zodiac. But its position in your birth chart reveals a great deal about the hidden or darker aspects of our character, and the tools at our disposal to bring them to light. Pluto shows where we plumb the depths of our own characters or experience – where we tear down what doesn't work for us and regenerate new life and energy. Pluto doesn't do things lightly. If there is something we have been hiding from or are afraid of, Pluto forces us to confront our demons. It's not a comfortable process but the changes Pluto enforces eventually bring us healing and self-forgiveness through understanding our less palatable emotions and aspects of ourselves.

> **Planetary ruler of:** Scorpio
>
> **Pluto keywords:** death, sex, transformation, regeneration, desire, power, destruction, obsession, secrets, hidden depths, insight

PLUTO IN THE BIRTH CHART

Pluto in Fire signs (Aries, Leo, Sagittarius):

Pluto Fire people transform in an impressive, creative, dramatic way. These individuals like being in charge and learn profound lessons from the effect their power has on others, or heal by realising the power others have on them.

Pluto in Earth signs (Taurus, Virgo, Capricorn):

Pluto Earth types transform and heal by turning old value systems on their head and creating better, new solutions that heal old wounds. Change is slow but permanent and enlightening.

Pluto in Air signs (Gemini, Libra, Aquarius):

Pluto Air types want to get to the bottom of how we think about things. They transform and heal by plundering their own psychological depths and making peace with any demons they encounter there – or by helping others deal with their own mental anguish.

Pluto in Water signs (Cancer, Scorpio, Pisces):

Pluto Water people often encounter a crisis where they are faced with their own repressed or hidden emotional depths – or have to deal with others' intense emotional dramas. Healing comes through acceptance, honesty and forgiveness.

PART 6

ASTROLOGY AND RELATIONSHIPS

The most accurate way to work out if people will get along is to analyse their unique birth charts using astrological techniques known as synastry or composite chart comparison. But the compatibility of the Sun signs involved is still fundamentally important because the Sun represents our basic ego - who we really are. Some signs of the zodiac get on better than others because they share similar traits and qualities - or, as with opposite signs of the zodiac, they mirror back to us what we need to explore in ourselves.

TRIPLICITIES, QUADRUPLICITIES AND POLARITIES

TRIPLICITIES – COMPATIBLE ELEMENT TYPES

Each sign has an elemental type (Fire, Earth, Air and Water) that they share with two other signs. The signs that share the same triplicity usually understand each other and get on well but they are also attracted to, or can learn from, their opposite element. As a rule, Fire signs sympathise with Air signs and Water signs sympathise with Earth signs.

FIRE SIGNS: ARIES, LEO, SAGITTARIUS

Compatible with Air signs

Fire signs are enthusiastic, spontaneous and active. They get bored with too much practical planning (Earth) or are uncomfortable emoting (Water). But they learn from applying more analysis (Air).

EARTH SIGNS: TAURUS, VIRGO, CAPRICORN

Compatible with Water signs

Earth signs are practical, stable and conservative. They're suspicious of too much spontaneity (Fire) or lack of practicality (Air) but empathise with the Water signs' understanding of emotion.

AIR SIGNS: GEMINI, LIBRA, AQUARIUS

Compatible with Fire signs

Air signs are intellectual, versatile and analytical. They feel burdened by Water signs' clingy emotions and annoyed by Earth's slowness to take action. But they learn from the Fire signs' assertiveness.

WATER SIGNS: CANCER, SCORPIO, PISCES

Compatible with Earth signs

Water signs are intuitive, emotional and imaginative. They distrust Fire signs' blunt approach and find Air's over intellectualising escapist waffle. But they understand Earth's need for structure and deliberation.

QUADRUPLICITIES AND POLARITIES

The zodiac is also divided into three groups of four signs known as quadruplicates that share the same qualities. These characteristics are named Cardinal, Fixed and Mutable and they are grouped as follows:

QUADRUPLICITIES

Cardinal: Aries, Libra, Cancer, Capricorn
Outgoing, creative and enterprising.

Fixed: Taurus, Scorpio, Leo, Aquarius
Stubborn or rigid in opinion or feelings.

Mutable: Gemini, Sagittarius, Virgo, Pisces
Flexible, versatile and tolerant.

POLARITIES

The six opposite zodiac signs are of the same
quadruplicity and each polarity reflects the need for
balance in particular areas of life:

Aries–Libra – the self versus the other (Cardinal).

Taurus–Scorpio – form versus transformation (Fixed).

Gemini–Sagittarius – details versus broad perspective
(Mutable).

Cancer–Capricorn – a private life versus a career (Cardinal).

Leo–Aquarius – self-expression versus being part of a group (Fixed).

Virgo–Pisces – order versus chaos (Mutable).

 **ARIES RELATIONSHIPS**

How Aries people relate to others in love and work.

Aries: Love
Aries people want someone who is as passionate and enthusiastic as they are in love. They need adventure and get bored easily. They don't want to talk about their feelings all the time – but they do enjoy an exuberant sex life and need an adventurous partner.

Best matches: Leo, Sagittarius and Libra
Worst matches: Taurus, Pisces

Aries: Work
Aries likes to be the boss and needs people who'll respect them as their leader. They like to take the initiative and expect others to be open and candid with their ideas, and free with their thoughts and creativity. They have oodles of respect for people who speak their mind and they expect others to listen when they speak theirs!

Best matches: Aries, Sagittarius, Gemini
Worst matches: Scorpio, Virgo

TAURUS RELATIONSHIPS

How Taurus people relate to others in love and work.

Taurus: Love
Taurus people don't dive into relationships without weighing up the consequences of their actions carefully. Once committed, they are ardent, loving and loyal partners who will move mountains for the people they love. Change can be upsetting, so they need someone who respects their need of routine and comfort.

Best matches: Cancer, Scorpio, Virgo
Worst matches: Leo, Aquarius

Taurus: Work
Taurus people are well-organised hard workers. They need structure and to know what they are expected to be doing on a day-to-day basis. They're not rule breakers and don't respond well to uncertainty. But when they feel secure and valued they will respond by being the most loyal boss or employee possible.

Best matches: Capricorn, Cancer, Taurus
Worst matches: Gemini, Aquarius

GEMINI RELATIONSHIPS

How Gemini people relate to others in love and work.

Gemini: Love

For Gemini love has to be communicated – without regular interaction and analysis of their thoughts and feelings Gemini can end up drawing their own assumptions and conclusions, which probably won't have much bearing on reality. Overwhelming emotions can scare Geminis, who prefer to rationalise their feelings. They need a partner who they can be honest with so there are no secrets blocking the flow of communication.

Best matches: Sagittarius, Libra, Leo
Worst matches: Taurus, Scorpio

Gemini: Work

Geminis aren't always the most practical of people at work but they're never short of a good idea. They can multi-task several different projects at once and think on as many different levels. They thrive on bouncing ideas off others, are excellent at making connections and make brilliant researchers.

Best matches: Libra, Aquarius, Virgo
Worst matches: Capricorn, Pisces

 ## CANCER RELATIONSHIPS

How Cancer people relate to others in love and work.

Cancer: Love

Cancer people radiate their nurturing vibes over their children, relatives, lovers and pets. Even plants do well if on the receiving end of a Cancerian's affections. Because they're so in tune with the emotional atmosphere they can be oversensitive and become hurt by any perceived criticism. If a Cancer person feels insecure or unloved they retreat into their shell until it's safe to come out.

Best matches: Capricorn, Pisces, Cancer
Worst matches: Aquarius, Leo

Cancer: Work

Cancerians are shrewd professionals, tenacious and intuitive. They can be a little defensive or self-effacing if asked to account for themselves, even if being asked to talk about their successes. They're usually happier to play a supporting role rather than being in the spotlight but deep down they know it's because of them that everything is a blinding success!

Best matches: Virgo, Libra, Scorpio
Worst matches: Gemini, Leo

 LEO RELATIONSHIPS

How Leo people relate to others in love and work.

Leo: Love

When a Leo's in love they want to sing it from the rooftops. Love fills them with hope and joy and they'll radiate it like their ruling planet, the Sun itself. Leo will place the person they adore at the centre of their universe but they will be very disappointed if the object of their affections doesn't reflect that love back to them as energetically as they insist.

Best matches: Aquarius, Libra, Sagittarius
Worst matches: Taurus, Capricorn

Leo: Work

Leos love to be the boss; it's just the natural order of the zodiac. It's where they're most comfortable and they will expect others to respect their authority. They're demanding but understanding of their colleagues and they expect recognition of a job well done. An under-appreciated Leo in the workplace is a sad sight indeed!

Best matches: Aries, Gemini, Taurus
Worst matches: Pisces, Virgo

 VIRGO RELATIONSHIPS

How Virgo people relate to others in love and work.

Virgo: Love

Modest Virgos approach passion with a little natural reserve but when they feel secure and cherished they blossom. Virgos are thoughtful, gentle lovers who notice even the smallest details of their partner's behaviour, which can be very endearing, but sometimes Virgo's questioning can become a little intense.

Best matches: Capricorn, Taurus, Pisces
Worst matches: Aries, Leo

Virgo: Work

If you want something done, ask a Virgo. Virgos are always busy – even when they really have nothing to do... there's always something to be scored off a list. Virgo characters are ruthlessly efficient, smart and studious at work – but stress can crop up if they don't make time for deliberate relaxation.

Best matches: Taurus, Gemini, Aries
Worst matches: Pisces, Leo

 LIBRA RELATIONSHIPS

How Libra people relate to others in love and work.

Libra: Love

Libra is the zodiac sign most associated with love and relationships and they are great romantics at heart. Sometimes they can be in love with the idea of love rather than the practical reality but Libra people will lavish their partner with real affection, warmth and emotion. Librans need to remember that they are independent human beings and not always thinking or acting as a 'unit'.

Best matches: Aries, Gemini, Taurus
Worst matches: Sagittarius, Virgo

Libra: Work

Above all Libra people need a harmonious work environment. They are skilled at getting along with all sorts of different people but they feel the strain when others are at loggerheads. Often their relationships with their colleagues are more important to them than the actual work itself.

Best matches: Leo, Gemini, Aries
Worst matches: Pisces, Leo

 SCORPIO RELATIONSHIPS

How Scorpio people relate to others in love and work.

Scorpio: Love

Scorpio has something of a sexy, ruthless reputation but only because they experience love in an intensely passionate way. Scorpios are experts at disguising their real feelings unless they have a partner they can really trust. They need someone who isn't frightened of real intimacy with whom they can share their deepest secrets and experiences.

Best matches: Scorpio, Cancer, Taurus
Worst matches: Leo, Gemini

Scorpio: Work

Scorpios have tremendous reserves of energy and when they enjoy their work they excel at it. But they need a satisfying career otherwise they can become very bored. All that passion for life has to go somewhere – so a fulfilling hobby could make a world of difference.

Best matches: Capricorn, Libra, Cancer
Worst matches: Leo, Aries

 SAGITTARIUS RELATIONSHIPS

How Sagittarius people relate to others in love and work.

Sagittarius: Love

Sagittarius individuals are very independent so when they fall in love it can be a little overwhelming. They're used to wanting space – not more closeness, so it can throw them a little off-balance. But when they see love as an adventure with new discoveries to make about their partner and themselves, they enter into the feeling whole- and open-heartedly.

Best matches: Leo, Libra, Aries
Worst matches: Capricorn, Taurus

Sagittarius: Work

Sagittarians are big thinkers. To hell with the details, they don't want to get weighed down with the practicalities. A predictable routine is not good for Sagittarians. They have real vision and energy to get their ideas off the ground but don't let them near a budget; they'll drain it before they even knew it existed.

Best matches: Taurus, Leo, Libra
Worst matches: Virgo, Pisces

CAPRICORN RELATIONSHIPS

How Capricorn people relate to others in love and work.

Capricorn: Love

Capricorns are not impulsive and they don't enter into relationships lightly. They can be extremely choosy because they know that if they decide to make a commitment to someone they will take their responsibility for that person's heart very seriously. Capricorns can seem aloof or reserved in love but this is mainly to cover up a natural shyness or uncertainty. They can feel very deeply hurt but you'd never know it. Capricorns and their partners benefit from being more demonstrative with each other to encourage emotional honesty and empathy.

Best matches: Virgo, Cancer, Pisces
Worst matches: Gemini, Leo

Capricorn: Work

Capricorns are the zodiac's most accomplished business people. They are shrewd, determined and ambitious and instinctively know how to get to the top of their chosen career. They are hard-working, practical and learn quickly from their mistakes and successes.

Best matches: Capricorn, Taurus, Cancer
Worst matches: Gemini, Aquarius

 ## AQUARIAN RELATIONSHIPS

How Aquarian people relate to others in love and work.

Aquarius: Love

Aquarians are fiercely independent and need partners who won't be too clingy or dependent upon them for emotional reassurance. Aquarians rebel against traditional roles and their love lives can be a little eccentric. But as long as intellectual rapport is present they make wise and exciting partners.

Best matches: Virgo, Cancer, Pisces
Worst matches: Gemini, Leo

Aquarius: Work

Original, progressive thinkers, Aquarians want to lead change. They make excellent politicians or spokespeople for those who find it difficult to speak up for themselves. Boredom is the enemy of the average Aquarian at work who won't relish the mundane day-to-day stuff – they need someone else to take care of the practicalities.

Best matches: Capricorn, Aries, Sagittarius
Worst matches: Leo, Pisces

 PISCES RELATIONSHIPS

How Pisces people relate to others in love and work.

Pisces: Love

Pisces are mysterious, compassionate, emotional people who live for romance but can spend as much time fantasising about love as actually doing something about finding it. When they discover someone special who feels as they do, they can create heaven on Earth together. But an occasional reality check with their partner wouldn't go amiss.

Best matches: Virgo, Scorpio, Cancer
Worst matches: Aquarius, Libra

Pisces: Work

Pisces are creative with rich imaginations and excel as artists, writers and musicians. They're not the most self-disciplined of people and will shy away from the limelight just when they need it most. Often just a little encouragement or belief from others gives all that's needed to help Pisces excel at what they do.

Best matches: Pisces, Aquarius, Scorpio
Worst matches: Taurus, Libra

Remember these relationship comparisons are based on Sun sign personality types. To include compatibility for the Moon, Rising signs and the rest of the planets would be a whole new book! So don't be disheartened if you come up as a 'worst match' with someone you get on with – your Sun sign is only one part of a complex story.

PART 7

ALL ABOUT BIRTH CHARTS

A personal birth chart, or horoscope, is a picture of what the heavens looked like when someone was born. The more accurate the time of birth, the more information you'll be able to discover about the person. Horoscopes can be drawn for the birth of an event, too. Birth charts are created to see what kind of planetary conditions were in operation at the start of wars, the crowning of a queen, the rise of a political movement or for when someone you know won the lottery. You can look at a horoscope for any moment for information about what is likely to happen, what did happen or what is happening now. Whether you are looking at the chart of a person or an event, horoscopes share the same characteristics.

THE TWELVE HOUSES

The 360-degree circle of the birth chart contains 12 sections known as houses. Each house governs a particular area of life as follows:

First house – associated with Aries

The self, appearance, identity, character

Second house – associated with Taurus

Money, talents, possessions, skills, income

Third house – associated with Gemini

Siblings, communication, short-distance travel, neighbours

Fourth house – associated with Cancer

The mother, home and domestic life, the past

Fifth house – associated with Leo

Love affairs, creativity, gambling, children

Sixth house – associated with Virgo

Health, routine work, pets, organisation

Seventh house – associated with Libra

Relationships, others, adversaries

Eighth house – associated with Scorpio

Sex, death, joint finances, the occult

Ninth house – associated with Sagittarius

Long-distance travel, education, faith

Tenth house – associated with Capricorn

Worldly success, career, father, ambitions

Eleventh house – associated with Aquarius

Friends, groups, movements, ideals

Twelfth house – associated with Pisces

Karma, spirituality, unconscious, dreams

THE FOUR ANGLES

The birth chart has four important points known as the Angles. The first is always the Ascendant - or Rising sign, the sign of the zodiac that was rising on the eastern horizon for the moment the person (or event) was born. The other angles are the Descendant, the Imum Coeli and the Medium Coeli - also known as the Midheaven.

Ascendant (AC) First house

This is the point most personally associated with the person - it's their Rising sign - the way they react to the world around them.

Imum Coeli (IC) Fourth house

Located in the southern point of the birth chart, this describes the person's home life, childhood, past and roots.

Descendant (DC) Seventh house

Always exactly opposite the Ascendant. This point signifies 'the other' and describes the type of relationships the person has.

Medium Coeli/Midheaven (MC)
Tenth house

The Midheaven is at the north of the horoscope and shows the person's worldly ambitions and opportunities for success.

THE SYMBOLS OF THE PLANETS, SIGNS AND ASPECTS

Each planet and sign has a glyph or symbol as follows:

Planets:

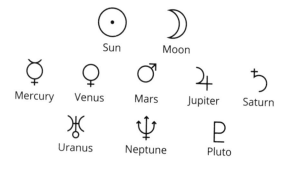

Sun   Moon

Mercury   Venus   Mars   Jupiter   Saturn

Uranus   Neptune   Pluto

Zodiac signs:

Aries   Taurus   Gemini   Cancer   Leo   Virgo

Libra   Scorpio   Sagittarius   Capricorn   Aquarius   Pisces

PLANETARY ASPECTS

The aspects are connections formed by the planets in the horoscope when they are at a particular distance from each other and they describe different types of energy. These are usually shown in symbol form in a separate grid next to the horoscope. But they also usually appear as lines criss-crossing the chart itself.

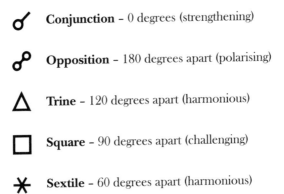

Conjunction – 0 degrees (strengthening)

Opposition – 180 degrees apart (polarising)

Trine – 120 degrees apart (harmonious)

Square – 90 degrees apart (challenging)

Sextile – 60 degrees apart (harmonious)

LOOKING AT AN EXAMPLE BIRTH CHART

BIRTH CHART for a person born on 1 May 1969 at 5:55 p.m. in Glasgow, Scotland, using the Equal House system.

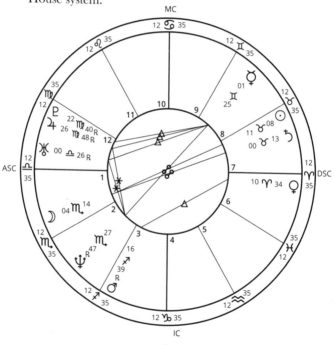

☉									
☍	☽								
		☿							
			♀						
			△	♂					
	△				♃				
	☍					♄			
	△			♂			⛢		
	☍			✳			✳	♆	
	△			♂			♂	✳	♇

ASPECTARIAN grid for the birth chart opposite, showing the aspects made by each planet

On the birth chart you'll see a circle with the 12 zodiac signs marked in their 30 degree sections, placed in a counter-clockwise direction around the edge of the outer circle. The exact positions for these are calculated using the Ascendant/Rising sign as the starting point. The Ascendant shows the sign and planets that were *ascending* or rising above the horizon when the person was born. This is seen as a vitally important place in the birth chart because symbolically it relates to the point where the Sun rises at dawn every morning, bringing its life-sustaining light to the planet.

In Western astrology the Rising sign is always depicted on the left-hand side of the chart not the right as it would be if looking at a map. This is because the chart is drawn from the perspective of the person being in the middle of the chart looking *out* rather than from the person looking down on the chart, so East and West are reversed as you look at them.

In the example chart you can note that at exactly 5.55 p.m. on 1 May 1969 in Glasgow, the sign rising on the eastern horizon was Libra – 12 degrees and 35 minutes of Libra to be exact. The Ascendant/Rising sign is always at the cusp (dividing line) of the First House – the part of the horoscope most associated with the self. From here the other 11 signs are drawn in a counter-clockwise direction until the circle is complete. The 12 inner segments of the chart are known as the houses. There are different house systems but the easiest to grasp is the Equal House system where they always remain in the same position – the first house always starts at the Ascendant. You can see their numbers in this example around the circle in the centre of the chart.

BASIC INTERPRETATION

THE PLANETS IN THE CHART

Looking at this birth chart we can see that this person was born with the sign of Libra on the eastern horizon – they have a Libra Ascendant/Rising sign. The Sun was in Taurus in the seventh house and the Moon was in the sign of Scorpio in the second house. Mercury was in Gemini in the eighth and Mars was in Sagittarius in the third house. Venus was in Aries in the sixth. Jupiter was in Virgo in the twelfth and Neptune was in Scorpio in the second. Uranus was in Libra in the twelfth and Pluto was also in the twelfth house, but in the sign of Virgo.

SUN, MOON AND RISING SIGN

So how do we start to recognise a person through all these symbols and signs? Starting with the Sun (core personality) in Taurus we can suppose this is a usually stable, reliable, patient person – perhaps someone who likes routine and can be a little stubborn. The Sun is in the seventh house, which is associated with Libra (relationships/balance and harmony) so there's a need to discover the self through interaction and experiences with others in order to feel 'whole'. These characteristics are further emphasised by the Moon (emotions) being located in Scorpio - Taurus's opposite sign. Taurus likes to build and stay secure while Scorpio prefers to tear things down or transform. So there ought to be something of a dichotomy present in this person's life. As the Ascendant/Rising sign (the persona one prefers to show the world) is in diplomatic, sociable Libra, this person wishes to be seen as pleasant, fair-minded and socially-aware, so they may find their emotions quite intrusive at times - especially as the Moon is in the first house ruling the appearance - this is someone who wears their heart on their sleeve, whether they wish to or not!

MERCURY, VENUS, MARS

In the example chart Mercury (communication) is in its own sign of Gemini which makes it a particularly strong planet. This could suggest a love of words, a writer or speaker, certainly someone with a restless mind or a great deal of mental activity. Because Mercury (thinking/communication) is in the eighth house (death/sex/deep emotions), there's a need to feel a mental connection with others on a profound level. Venus (love/beauty) in Aries can be dynamic, childish, brave and impulsive - and in the sixth house (Virgo/health/routine) may suggest someone who needs to make their daily routine beautiful in some way, and who enjoys detailed work. Mars (the desire to act) in Sagittarius shows an outgoing, enthusiastic approach to life and in the third house (Gemini/communication) can be philosophical, clever or broad minded.

JUPITER, SATURN

Jupiter (expansion/luck) is in Virgo (methodical, detail-oriented) which indicates a realistic approach but can also symbolise someone who spends too long getting the details right on large projects. Jupiter in the twelfth house (Pisces/unconscious/psychic) could indicate someone with a boundless imagination. Saturn (restriction) is in Taurus (stable, secure) in the seventh house (Libra/relationships), which might mean this person feels comfortable with an older partner, or perhaps has had to deal with challenging conditions in a long-term relationship.

URANUS, NEPTUNE, PLUTO

Uranus (change/rebellion) in Libra (relationships/balance) in the twelfth house (dreams/spirituality) suggests an individual who has an unconventional and psychic connection with the people closest to them. They have a fascination with the supernatural, experience vivid or unusual dreams and can suffer with sleep problems or embody an inner restlessness that's hard to pin down. With Neptune (imagination/loss) in Scorpio (powerful emotion) this person would probably have an intense imagination, and in the second house (Taurus/money/talents) it would indicate an impractical approach to money or at least some difficulty in holding onto what they own. Or, alternatively, Neptune in the second shows artistic skills and abilities that could form a lucrative income. Pluto (transformation) in Virgo (organised, details) describes a person that likes to clear up a mess and in the twelfth house (Pisces/dreams) they would benefit from self-analysis or 'tidying up' of their own subconscious realms. They'd make an excellent psychotherapist.

ASPECTS IN THE EXAMPLE CHART

The grid on the page opposite the birth chart shows the planetary aspects – the angles formed by each planet to one another. These are shown as criss-crossing lines in the centre of the birth chart. The main aspects in the example chart are:

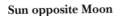

Sun opposite Moon

Sun (core character) polarising the Moon (emotions).

Moon opposite Saturn

Moon (emotions) polarising Saturn (restriction).

Venus trine Mars

Venus (love/beauty) harmonising with Mars (desire for action).

Neptune sextile Uranus, Jupiter and Pluto

Neptune (intuition) harmonising with Uranus (change), Jupiter (luck/expansion) and Pluto (transformation).

Mercury trine Uranus, Jupiter and Pluto

Mercury (communication) harmonising with Uranus (change), Jupiter (luck/expansion) and Pluto (transformation).

Neptune opposite Mercury

Neptune (intuition) opposes Mercury (communication).

Jupiter conjunct Uranus and Pluto

Jupiter (luck/expansion), Uranus (change) and Pluto (transformation) are all strengthened. When three or more planets are sitting next to each other it is known as a 'stellium' and it concentrates the energy on the house or sign/signs they occupy.

A TOOL FOR SELF-DISCOVERY

Astrology is a vast subject and is as complex as the psychology of the person whose chart you're looking at. The above interpretation is an extremely simplified account to give an idea of where to begin. You can look at your own horoscope for years and still be inspired by the depth of insight it offers. It's good to remember that no planet, sign or aspect in a chart is all 'good' or 'bad' – it's all about blending the energies to paint a more complete picture. What you see in a birth chart doesn't necessarily describe who you are right now, but it does represent challenges, opportunities and issues that you will encounter at some point in your life – dormant energies waiting for the right transit to trigger them into life.

NOW LOOK AT YOUR OWN BIRTH CHART

To get a free copy of your own birth chart, visit the Astrodienst website at: www.astro.com, click the Free Horoscopes link on the blue top bar, then click the Drawings & Calculations section and Natal Chart, Ascendant. After this it should take you to a page where it asks you to enter your birth information. If you don't know your birth time put 12.00 midday, which will at least give you a chart for your birthday with accurate positions for most of the planets. But remember that to find your true Ascendant/Rising sign you'll need as exact a time as possible.

CONCLUSION

Now it's time to use astrology to draw your own conclusions about who you are as a person and how you relate to the people around you. You might begin by learning more about your Sun sign to give your daily newspaper horoscope more depth and insight. But if, for example, you wish to know why you never get along with your boss or why you always attract oddballs – and what to do about those situations – you'll be continually impressed by astrology's revealing and rewarding answers. How exciting to be at the start of such a fascinating journey – may the stars be your mirror!

RESOURCES

FANTASTICALLY HELPFUL WEBSITES:

astro.com – world-renowned astrologers Liz Greene and Robert Hand founded this awesome resource for both experienced astrologers and complete beginners. It's free to sign up and obtain your birth chart and personalised daily horoscopes. You can also spend time looking at the detailed relationship charts and Extended Chart Selection, and share your questions and knowledge with likeminded types on their information-packed forum.

newparadigmastrology.com – astrologer and all-round wise soul Kaypacha posts thought-provoking, heart-warming videos examining the current astrological climate in detail.

linda-goodman.com – a densely packed forum dedicated to late astrologer, writer and poet Linda Goodman. You need to register if you want to post but the site itself is an inexhaustible resource where people from all walks of life share their own astrological experience.

astrologyzone.com – astrologer Susan Miller writes warm, but incredibly detailed and consistent monthly horoscopes as well as providing useful sections for beginners new to the subject.

WONDERFUL ASTROLOGY BOOKS:

There are hundreds of astrology books out there but here are a few of my favourites:

Parker, Derek and Julia *Parkers' Astrology* (1994, Dorling Kindersley)

Goodman, Linda *Sun Signs* (1999, Pan)

Mann, A. T. *The Round Art* (2003, Vega Books)

Pelletier, Robert *Planets in Aspect* (1987, Schiffer Publishing)

Birkbeck, Lyn *The Instant Astrologer* (2003, O Books)

Greene, Liz *Astrology for Lovers* (1999, Thorsons)

ABOUT THE AUTHOR

Marion Williamson is an astrologer, writer and editor. She became curious about the stars after her mum taught her how to recognise the constellations in the night sky. When she was a teenager she discovered an enchanting stash of very old library books on astrology, which she still hasn't returned. She got hooked on drawing up birth charts and funded her way through university by having astrology articles published in the national press. From 2000 to 2010 she was the deputy editor, then the editor, of *Prediction* magazine, the UK's original spiritual lifestyle publication (1936–2012). While there she interviewed and worked with many of the world's leading astrologers and self-development experts. Marion is a well-known contributor to a diverse range of books, magazines and publications in the Mind, Body, Spirit world. She lives with Tim and their cat, Paddy, in Brighton. To find out more visit: marionwilliamson.com or check out her Twitter @_I_Am_Astrology.

ASTROLOGY IS A LANGUAGE. IF YOU UNDERSTAND, THE SKY SPEAKS TO YOU.

DANE RUDHYAR

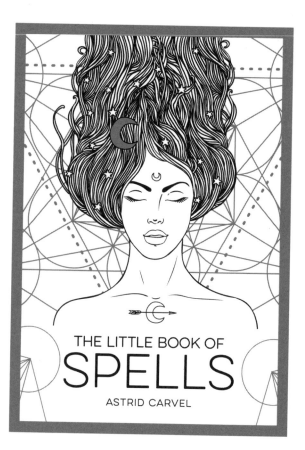

THE LITTLE BOOK OF
SPELLS

ASTRID CARVEL

THE LITTLE BOOK OF SPELLS

Astrid Carvel

ISBN: 978-1-78685-799-6

Paperback

£6.99

Discover the techniques for performing white witchcraft with this beginner's guide to casting spells. Learn the importance of the moon's cycles and ways to tap into the rhythms of the natural world, and how to source your own ingredients. From love potions using candle magic and rituals for attracting prosperity, to charm bags for courage and incantations for lasting happiness, there is a spell for every occasion.

If you're interested in finding out more
about our books, find us on Facebook at
Summersdale Publishers and follow us
on Twitter at **@Summersdale**.

WWW.SUMMERSDALE.COM

IMAGE CREDITS

pp.4–5, 9 – celestial symbols © Sudowoodo/Shutterstock.com
p.11 and throughout – moon © Tatiana Apanasova/Shutterstock.com
p.19 – mandala © Panptys/Shutterstock.com
p.21 – alchemy symbols © Panptys/Shutterstock.com
p.25 – ram's head © Helen Lane/Shutterstock.com
pp.24–36 – constellations © djgis/Shutterstock.com
pp.63–81 – planets © Firejackal/Shutterstock.com
pp.89–101 – zodiac symbols © painter/Shutterstock.com
p.110 – planet symbols © Peter Hermes Furian/Shutterstock.com;
zodiac icons © Brothers Good/Shutterstock.com